Introduction

"Hi! I'm **Colleen the Cat.** I love to read and learn. I'd like to introduce you to some of my buddies, who are in the hospital getting well. They're brave, beautiful and bookworms like me! Let's go!"

These Bookworm Buddies are amazing!

- Many were born early (before 9 months of their mom's pregnancy) and had to stay in the hospital for a long time. That's brave!

- Children born early can have injuries to all parts of their bodies, most often their lungs, intestines, or brains.

- To stay healthy, children with these kinds of injuries may need help to eat or breathe using special tubes and machines that you'll see in this book.

- Even as they get bigger and stronger, when they get sick, children with these health challenges often need to stay in the hospital, sometimes for weeks.

- No matter what help they need, reading books is a perfect way for Bookworm Buddies to spend time with loved ones, feel better and have fun!

A

A is for Amir – he's adorable, don't you agree?
"Mommy's soothing voice is the best medicine for me."

Amir loves listening to stories on his mom's lap–they make him sleepy!

B is for Bell. "Reading books feeds my heart,
as I bond with my buddy – we're rarely apart."

Bell is reading while she eats
through a special tube.
She's feeding her brain and body!

C

C is for cute, curious Cayden; hands-on is his style.
"Cuddling with mommy always makes me smile."

Cayden is having so much fun reading with his mom – he wants to help turn the pages!

D

With his dear, doting mama, D is for Dane.
"Sharing books helps develop my dazzling brain!"

Dane is looking and listening
as his mom reads a story.
This helps him learn!

E

E is for Evangeline; she enjoys every letter.
"When you read to me, your voice helps me feel better."

Evangeline is *enchanted* by her mom's kind face and voice!

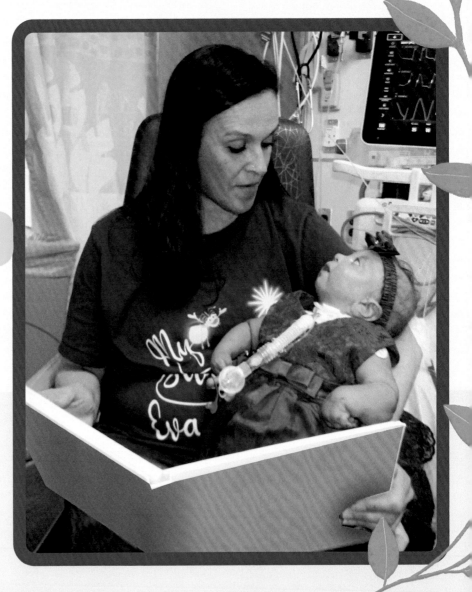

F

F is for Fallyn; she's fearless fun and more.
"Reading sets my imagination free to explore."

Even with a mask on her face, Fallyn is focused on her book – she loves reading!

G

G is for Grant and his sweet Grandpa, too.
"Reading is grand when I snuggle with you."

Reading is fun with the whole family: grandparents, sisters, brothers, aunts, uncles – everyone!

Hi is for nurse Hiba, with Derrionna in her care.
"There are so many happy stories that we can share."

Hiba is a nurse and helps take care of Derrionna. They're snuggled up for a story while she's in the hospital!

Medical Family

I

I is for Issac, who loves to look, listen and touch.
"When you share stories with me, I don't worry so much."

Issac is a good listener. He feels safe and loved on his mom's lap as she reads to him in the hospital!

J

J is for Javion; words and pictures are just right.
"They help me imagine places that are joyful and bright."

Javion is wearing blue glasses so he can see his book better – aren't they great?

K

**K is for Karlee; that's Chevy, her kind K-9 friend.
"I read and he listens, from the beginning to the end."**

Karlee is reading to a dog – that's so fun!
Pets love snuggling and listening to stories.

L

L is for Lily, bold and lovely like a flower.
"My dad's voice helps me bloom with *super story power!*"

Lily is listening to her dad read as he shows her the pictures. He is her superhero!

M

M is for Messiah and his merry mama – look!
"Happiness is mutual when we share a book."

Messiah is looking at his mom's face as she reads – they're so happy. The story is music to his ears!

N

**N is for Noe'Lynn, newly born but growing strong.
"My mom's my best teacher, nurturing me along."**

Noe'Lynn is dressed for story time.
Her mom takes such good care of her!

O

O is for baby Ocean; he's deep, strong and brave.
"Reading on mom's lap helps calm my stormy waves."

Ocean is a baby and a good listener.
Look how calm he is during the story!

P

P is for Penelope, a petite and perfect sweet-pea.
"Sunny stories with my mom are so peaceful to me."

Penelope loves her mom's smiling face.
It's like sunshine to help her grow!

Q is for questions; for quizzical Gabe these abound.
"I ask and mom answers, or the other way around."

Gabe and his mom love to talk
when they read together.
They're curious, like me!

R

R is for reading, robe and Amani's favorite color, red.
"It's what I love to do each night before retiring to bed."

Amani loves to read at bedtime;
it helps her sleep. Sweet dreams!

S is for Sammy, so sassy, strong and smart.
"I love sharing stories that touch my soul and heart."

Sammy loves reading to his friends.
One has a tracheostomy like he does!

T

**T is for Tali, with a bow tied around her head.
"My bond with you tightens with each story read."**

Sharing stories is a perfect way for Tali and her mom to bond!

BONDS

**U is for Us; Ja'Ceila and her devoted mom and dad.
"We read as a family– hearing your voices makes me glad."**

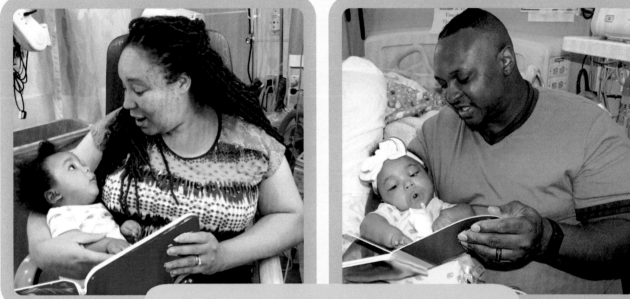

Ja'Celia's mom and dad love to read with her no matter where they are – what a *love-ly* reading family!

V is for valiant Vyren, who loves to read and learn.
"Pictures to see, words to try, pages to touch and turn!"

Vyren is a hands-on person. He learns by holding and exploring his book!

W

W is for **wonder** on Derrian's face when he reads.
"Books that are *interesting* are just what I need."

Derrian loves reading books about wrestling. There are books about so many fun and interesting things!

X

X is for eXtraordinary **Kenny and his kind reading crew.**
"My eXemplary hospital family loves reading with me, too!"

Kenny is reading with a nurse from his medical team and hospital family!

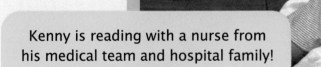

SHAPES
PETS

Y

Y is for **YOU**, Mika; perfect just as you are.
"Reading helps me feel strong and to shine like a star!"

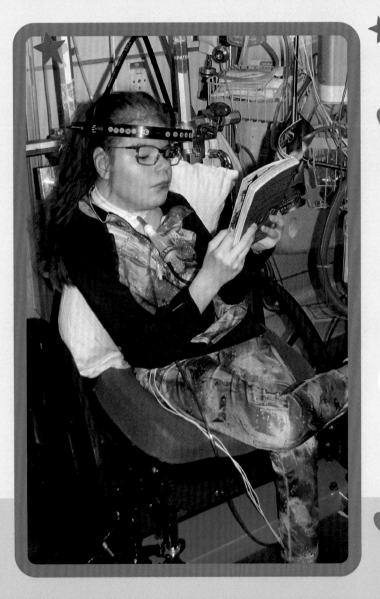

Mika is wearing a medical device that looks like a crown. Reading helps people shine like royalty!

Z

Z is for Ziva, who's catching ZZZs as her story is read.
"My mom and dad read to me when it's time for bed."

Ziva loved her story so much she fell asleep!

Goodnight, Bookworm Buddies!

Glossary

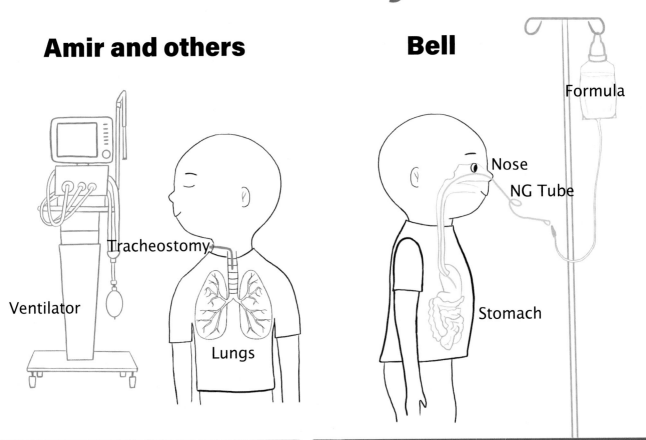

Amir and others

Ventilator

Tracheostomy

Lungs

Bell

Formula

Nose

NG Tube

Stomach

- When their lungs or throat are injured, children may need help to breathe.

- A tube brings air to and from a **ventilator** machine through a hole in the neck called a **tracheostomy.**

- A tracheostomy is made by **surgeons** and is sometimes permanent or can be closed when the child gets bigger.

- **NG** stands for **Naso-Gastric tube**

- **Naso** means "nose" and **Gastric** means "stomach."

- An **NG tube** goes through the nose down the throat and into the stomach or intestines to deliver liquid food and medicine.

- Some children need this when it's hard to swallow or digest solid food.

Fallyn

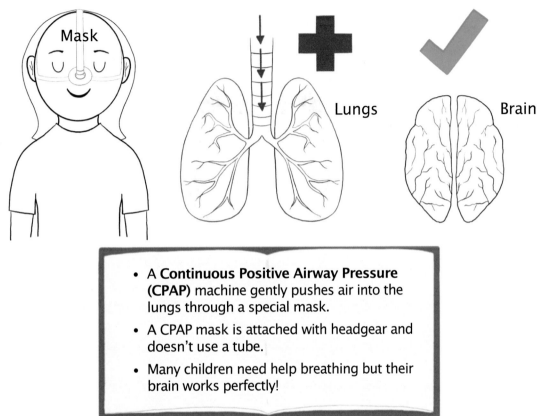

- A **Continuous Positive Airway Pressure (CPAP)** machine gently pushes air into the lungs through a special mask.
- A CPAP mask is attached with headgear and doesn't use a tube.
- Many children need help breathing but their brain works perfectly!

Lily and Others

- Because of a brain injury when she was a baby, Lily's body is stiff and she has trouble sitting up.
- Different parts of the brain control movement and language. So Lily listens lying down!

Brain

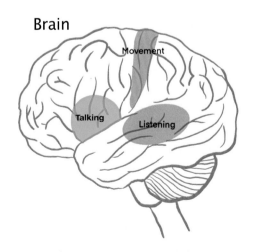

Amani

- The clear tube on Amani's face is called a **nasal cannula**. Extra oxygen flows through it as she breathes.

- **Nasal** means "nose"

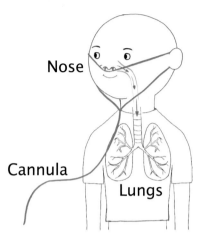

Sammy

- The blue piece on Sammy's tracheostomy is a **Passi Muir valve**.

- This valve lets air flow in but not out and helps him speak and swallow.

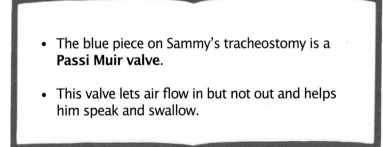

Mika

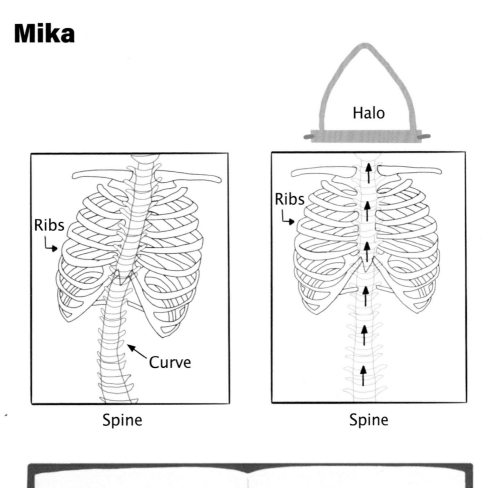

- **Scoliosis** is a condition where the spine is curved too much, which can hurt and make it hard to breathe.

- Mika is having a procedure called **halo gravity traction** that gently stretches and straightens the spine.

- The halo is attached to the head (skull) with small pins.

Text copyright 2023 by Dr. John Hutton and Amy McGrory
Photographs copyright 2023 by Amy McGrory
Illustrations copyright 2023 by Marci Chorpash
Layout Design by Mayte Suarez

Published by blue manatee press, Cincinnati, Ohio.
blue manatee press and associated logo
are registered trademarks of Arete Ventures, LLC.

First Edition: December 2023.

Library of Congress Cataloging-In-Publication Data
Bookworm Buddies / by Dr. John Hutton and Amy McGrory;
Illustrated by Marci Chorpash —1 st Ed.

Summary: A celebration of the healing power of reading in the hospital,
featuring children with complex health needs. Simple rhymes and color photographs
introduce these amazing children from A to Z, reading with family, medical caregivers,
pets and by themselves. Commentary provided by Colleen the Cat and her pal
Bookworm notes benefits of reading, especially to help children feel safe and loved. An
illustrated glossary describes medical devices required by these children. Ages 3 and up.

ISBN-13 (paperback): 979-8-9886382-1-6
1. Juvenile Nonfiction / Concepts / Alphabet.
2. Family & Relatioships / Children with Special Needs.

Printed in the USA.

The text for this book was set in Adobe InDesign.
Artwork was created digitally.